What's so special about autism?

Lorna Wing

The National
Autistic Society

First published 2006 by The National Autistic Society
393 City Road, London EC1V 1NG
www.autism.org.uk
www.info.autism.org.uk

ISBN 1 899280 99 5
      978 1 899280 99 5

Designed by Cottier & Sidaway

Printed by Newnorth Print

Contents

Introduction

This booklet describes the special problems which people with autism may face and the type of help they need. It discusses the underlying causes of autism; the evolution of ideas about autism; the clinical features; the special needs of people with these conditions and ways of helping; prevalence and the implications for services. The aim is to highlight the ways in which autistic spectrum disorders are different from other types of disabilities and the implications this has for services.

Since the 1960s, The National Autistic Society (NAS) in the UK and other locally based autism societies have provided a range of specialised services, including education and support for children and adults across the whole spectrum of autism. Their experience and expertise together with the invaluable insights of people with autism and their families is reflected in this booklet.

About the terminology used in this book

This booklet uses the terms 'autism' or 'autistic spectrum disorder' and the abbreviation 'ASD' to cover the whole range of developmental disorders, including Kanner autism and Asperger syndrome. However, where it refers to Asperger syndrome alone, the information given relates specifically to those who have been given this diagnosis.

The text occasionally uses the term 'his' when referring to a person with autism, but the information given can apply to any person with an autistic spectrum disorder.

A history of autism

- Autistic spectrum disorders (ASDs) result from an unusual pattern of brain development, in most cases beginning before birth or during the early years of childhood, which has lifelong effects.
- Complex genetic factors are the major cause in the great majority of people who are affected.
- In a minority, the autistic disorder is associated with pre-, peri- or post- natal conditions causing brain pathology, for example, tuberous sclerosis, fragile X, encephalitis complicating an infectious illness.
- Many 'syndromes' have been suggested but the criteria overlap with each other.
- The term 'autistic spectrum disorder' covers all clinical pictures that include a triad of impairments of social interaction, social communication and social imagination.

The concept of autism and the autistic spectrum is of comparatively recent origin, as is understanding of the problems and of the specialised help people with autism may need.

Descriptions of individuals with behaviour resembling autistic spectrum disorders can be found in historical literature. In the first part of the 20th century, the terms 'childhood psychosis' or 'childhood schizophrenia' were used to describe various patterns of unusual behaviour. In 1943, Leo Kanner was the first to adopt the name 'autism' to denote a particular small sub-group of these children.

In 1980, the term 'pervasive developmental disorder' (PDD)[1] was introduced for autism and related conditions. This has been widely used, particularly in America. Most workers in the field welcome the view that these conditions are developmental but many consider that the word 'pervasive' is not satisfactory, because most people with autistic disorders have 'patchy' profiles of skills and disabilities, in other words, they may be very capable in some areas, but do poorly in others.

Over the years various attempts have been made to define specific syndromes among children with unusual behaviour dating from infancy or early childhood. Between 1908 and 2002 at least 15 syndromes have been suggested in published literature. The two best-known and most frequently used to date are childhood autism, based on the descriptions by Leo Kanner, published in 1943, and Asperger syndrome, based on descriptions by Hans Asperger, published in German in 1944. Various other writers have also published their own criteria for autism and Asperger syndrome[2].

There are problems with all these so-called syndromes and sets of criteria. First, they depend on descriptions of behaviour, which are notoriously difficult to operationalise. Second, all the syndromes overlap with each other. Third, they also overlap with a range of general and specific developmental, behavioural and psychiatric conditions. Research

---

[1] American Psychiatric Association (1980). *Diagnostic and statistical manual* (DSM-III). Washington, D.C.: APA Press (subsequently used in DSM-III-Revised and the current DSM-IV); see also World Health Organization (1992). *International classification of diseases 10th edition ICD-10*. Geneva: World Health Organization

[2] American Psychiatric Association (2000). *Diagnostic and statistical manual* (DSM-IV) (4th ed. text revision). Washington, D.C.: APA Press; World Health Organization (1993). *ICD-10 classification of mental and behavioural disorders. Diagnostic criteria for research*. Geneva: World Health Organization

workers have tried to improve diagnosis of sub-groups by devising checklists, questionnaires and structured interview schedules but, as hands-on workers in the field know only too well, major problems remain.

The autistic spectrum

In a series of studies beginning in the 1970s, Wing and Gould tried to make sense of conflicting ideas on autistic disorders. On the basis of an epidemiological study of children under 15 and follow-up studies since then, they put forward the hypothesis of an autistic spectrum. This covers all the suggested syndromes and other behaviour patterns that include various mixtures of features from them.

What holds the spectrum together is an underlying combination of impairments of three aspects of child development, known as the 'triad of impairments'. This triad comprises impairments of social interaction, social communication and social imagination. Different people are affected in widely differing ways. Some are profoundly disabled while, at the other end of the scale, the most able people can become independent in living and working and a few have been recognised as having exceptional ability in the arts or sciences. The concept of the autistic spectrum recognises this, and the term autistic spectrum disorder is now widely used.

Features of autism

Impairment of social interaction

- The fundamental impairment underlying all the other problems is the lack of the biological social instinct that, in typical development, is present from birth.
- There is little or no understanding of the unwritten rules of social interaction.
- There is little or no empathy with other people and little or no understanding of other people's thoughts, feelings or psychological reactions.
- The result is a kind of innocent egocentricity.

Everyone with an autistic spectrum disorder, whatever their level of ability in other areas, has specific problems in coping with everyday life. The most fundamental of the impairments making up the triad is that affecting social interaction. This is the problem that makes autism so special. As Darwin pointed out, it is necessary for the survival of a species that its members recognise, respond to and communicate with each other from birth. Human babies are, virtually from the time they are born, aware of and interested in other humans. But those with autistic spectrum disorders lack this instinctive interest and responsiveness from birth, or lose it in almost all cases in their very early years. The most severely affected remain aloof and indifferent to others throughout their lives.

However, the majority, to varying degrees, gradually become aware that they are affected by other people, though the effects are often unwelcome. They have major problems in following the subtle and infinitely variable unwritten rules that govern social life. Those who are more able do gradually learn, through intellectual effort, at least some of these rules. However, in the absence or impairment of the social instinct, people with autistic spectrum disorders see everything from their own point of view. They are basically egocentric, not because they are deliberately nasty and selfish, but because they cannot help it.

Some people with autism try hard to fit in to their social group, but their close acquaintances usually become aware of the fact that they are different. Children who are not socially impaired are quick to recognise the odd one out. This makes the child with an autistic spectrum disorder in a mainstream school a target for bullying. Teachers who are unaware or dismissive of the problems of a child with an autistic spectrum disorder can also make life very difficult, especially if the child makes socially inappropriate remarks in class, apparently challenging the teacher's authority.

Impairment of social communication

- Impairment of the innate, biologically driven need to communicate.
- Difficulty with understanding verbal and non-verbal communication.
- Difficulty with using verbal and non-verbal communication.
- Difficulty in understanding the messages other people wish to convey when these are not fully verbalised.
- Special difficulty in taking part in reciprocal conversation.

Impairment of communication in people with autism, which affects both verbal and non-verbal aspects, varies from no communication at all to fluent, grammatical speech that is used mainly or only to talk about their own special interests. Communication problems are obvious among those who are more disabled. Even if they have some speech this is often idiosyncratic in form. It seems that they do not realise that speech and non-verbal communication can affect other people in useful ways. For example, there are stories of children with the ability to speak, who have been accidentally shut in somewhere but who never used their speech to call for help, despite being very distressed.

Communication difficulties tend to be less obvious among the more able people. Good grammatical speech can draw attention away from problems of comprehension, a tendency to literal interpretation and inappropriate vocal intonation. In educational assessments, individuals with superficially 'good' expressive language tend to be regarded as much more able than they really are, while the abilities of those with poorly developed speech may be underestimated.

At all levels of ability there is a special problem in verbalising feelings and emotional states. There is no doubt that basic emotions, such as sadness, happiness, anger and fear, are experienced by people with autistic spectrum disorders, but most are unable to express their feelings in words, even if they have good vocabularies.

So much of our everyday communication is not put into words but is conveyed by the immediate context, shared past experiences and non-verbal signals like tone of voice, facial expression, gestures and so on. These are a closed book to people with autistic spectrum disorders, further limiting their ability to 'read' other people, understand their intentions and engage easily in conversation.

Impairment of social imagination

- Difficulty in predicting the consequences of actions.
- Inability to imagine what goes on in other people's minds.

In children, impairment of imagination can affect the way they develop, significantly the way they use play to do this. Children with autism may not engage in any pretend play or if they do, it can be repetitive in form and involves others, if at all, only to do the bidding of the child concerned.

In some older children and adults their inner world is limited entirely to their own narrow interests. In others, it takes the form of an elaborate fantasy world that is repetitive with little or no social content. In yet others it can be repetitive acting out of roles, copied from real or fictional people, animals, or even inanimate objects such as trains. Whatever the form of the impairment of imagination, the effect is to impair the person's ability to appreciate the possible consequences of their own actions – that is, the ability to imagine 'What if?' This includes the impairment of the ability to imagine what other people are thinking and feeling. They lack a 'theory of mind'[3], the early beginnings of which are seen from around 18 months in typically developing children.

Repetitive patterns of activities

- New events are frightening because they are unpredictable.
- Safety is sought in repeating the same actions and resisting change.

The narrow, repetitive pattern of activities associated with the triad of impairments varies from simple, repetitive bodily movements, such as flapping hands and arms, jumping up and down and spinning round, to absorption in specific intellectual interests. People with autistic spectrum disorders, to varying degrees, find it difficult to cope with change in their preferred activities. They tend to react with distress to unexpected events, even if seemingly trivial – for example, if an activity that usually begins at 10am is, without warning, postponed until 11am, or if a child's bedtime routine is changed in one small detail.

Other people are especially unpredictable to those with autism, and therefore especially frightening. For example, people change the details of their appearance, their facial expressions, the things they say, their emotions, and the way in which they react to the same things on different days. All these aspects of typical human behaviour are baffling to people with autistic spectrum disorders.

Unusual responses to sensations

- Oversensitivity to various kinds of sensory input, particularly sounds and touch, is common.

In addition to the features appearing in diagnostic criteria for autistic spectrum disorders there are others that are also particularly characteristic. Difficulties caused by oversensitivity to various kinds of sensory input, particularly sounds and touch, are common. This sensory sensitivity may present in one of two ways.

Firstly, there may be a typical pain response and the person concerned may react with evident distress and withdrawal from the source of the sensation. Covering ears in response to noises is characteristic.

[3]Frith, U. (2003). *Autism: explaining the enigma*. 2nd edition. Oxford: Blackwell
Baron-Cohen, S. (1991). The theory of mind deficit in autism: how specific is it? *British Journal of Developmental Psychology*, 9, pp301-314
Baron-Cohen, S. (1991). The development of theory of mind in autism: deviance and delay. *Psychiatric Clinics of North America*, 14 (1), pp33-51

Secondly, there may be an inability to 'filter' noise, light or other activity in the environment. For example, an inability to filter sound may mean that background noise distracts or completely overwhelms the person. Bright daylight or the flickering of fluorescent lighting can also cause problems. Some react with aggression to others or self-injury, such as biting the back of the wrist. They may develop a long-lasting fear of places, people or objects they associate with the cause of the sensation that upsets them.

Problems with movement, gait and posture

- Impairments of motor co-ordination (dyspraxia) are common.
- Catatonic and parkinsonian features develop in around one in ten individuals during or after adolescence.

Some individuals are poorly co-ordinated in large or fine movements, or both, even if they have skill in one specific area, such as playing a musical instrument. Follow-up of children with autistic spectrum disorders into adolescence and adult life has revealed a problem that may appear with increasing age. This is the development of difficulties affecting movement, posture and speech, which affects around 10 per cent or more and can be found in individuals of any level of ability. These features are closely similar to aspects of catatonia and of parkinsonism. They include, among many others, increasing slowness; difficulty in crossing lines and going through doorways; inability to start actions and then to stop once started; peculiarities of gait; odd postures, especially of the hands and arms; staring, rapid blinking and facial grimaces; and reduction or cessation of speech, although marked echolalia (copying other people's speech) may remain. These problems may occur in brief or longer episodes, or they may be chronic and long-lasting. They appear to be a response to stress and high anxiety.

Unusual psychological profiles

- Patchy profiles on psychological testing are common.

If they are given psychological tests, it is often found that people with autistic spectrum disorders have very patchy profiles. That is, they may do well in some areas, such as number work, music, or visuo-spatial skills, but poorly in others, such as comprehension of language. Less often, language skills are better than non-verbal abilities.

A small proportion of people with autism, although they have severe learning disabilities, have some outstanding gift, perhaps in music, mathematical calculations, drawing or memory – for example, being able to name species of dinosaurs or past members of football teams. These are the so-called 'autistic savants'. Those who are high-functioning can also have big discrepancies between different types of skills. A special skill may be the basis of a special interest. Any type of profile may be found, but patchiness is particularly characteristic of autistic disorders.

Problems affecting behaviour

- To a person with an autistic spectrum disorder, the world is a chaotic muddle. This can result in challenging behaviour.
- Depression or other psychiatric illnesses are common.
- Motor co-ordination problems may be exacerbated.

The experience of an unpredictable, chaotic world has been well described by a number of high-functioning people who have written books about their experiences (see the 'Further reading' section on page 30). Because the social world is so hard for them to understand, people with autistic spectrum disorders tend to be very anxious in social situations. They may react with challenging behaviour such as aggression to others – particularly those they see as the agents of unwelcome change – destructiveness or self-injury. Alternatively, they may turn inwards, not responding to other people at all or communicating with the world around them. The more able people, who become aware that they are different from most other people, may develop psychiatric illnesses. Depression is particularly common.

Two particular aspects of the overall clinical picture, if one or both are present, make accurate diagnosis more difficult but provision of special help just as important as for any other manifestation of autism. One is the association of an autistic spectrum disorder with attention deficit and hyperactive disorder (ADHD). The other is association with the behaviour pattern described by Elizabeth Newson[4], which she calls pathological demand avoidance (PDA). Children with PDA typically resist doing what others ask them to do and they also seem to find pleasure and reward in causing distress to other people. For both these clinical pictures an organised daily programme of activities has to be planned for each individual. To be successful, this requires considerable experience with these conditions and detailed understanding of the child or adult concerned.

Although the great majority of people with autistic spectrum disorders are law-abiding, a tiny minority get into trouble with the law. This is more likely to happen with those who have PDA. Examples of behaviour which might get them into trouble are stealing objects related to special interests, aggressive responses to being bullied at school, or harassment of people they especially like or dislike. Individuals in this tiny sub-group are usually aware of the law but tend to feel that it does not apply to them.

[4]Newson, E., Le Marechal, K., and David, C. (2003). Pathological demand avoidance syndrome: a necessary distinction within the pervasive developmental disorders. *Archives of Disease in Childhood*, 88, pp595-600

Understanding the special needs

- It is important that the special needs of people with autistic spectrum disorders are recognised by service providers.

As a result of their special problems in understanding and coping with the world, people with autistic spectrum disorders have special needs that are, in many important ways, different from those of people with other disabilities. This is why appropriate service provision is so important. Providing the right kind of help in an appropriate environment with an appropriate programme of activities is the most effective way of minimising or preventing challenging behaviour.

The need for early diagnosis

- Recognition and diagnosis of the nature of the autistic spectrum disorder as early in life as possible is the essential first step in helpful intervention.
- It is equally important to recognise the presence of an autistic spectrum disorder when associated with other developmental, physical, psychological, or psychiatric conditions.

The essential first step towards meeting special needs is that the autistic spectrum disorder is recognised and diagnosed, preferably as early in life as possible. Originally, Kanner thought that autism was a unique syndrome, separate from all other conditions. This idea coloured attitudes to diagnosis for many years. Now it is known that the triad of impairments can occur on its own or in association with other developmental, physical, psychological or psychiatric disorders. This makes for major problems in recognising the presence of an autistic disorder.

Another type of misdiagnosis occurs when an autistic spectrum disorder is mistaken for another developmental disorder. Delay in language development, poor motor co-ordination or poor reading can all occur as part of the autistic picture and may be assumed to be the only problem in the child concerned. Diagnostic expertise lies in recognising the presence of the underlying triad of impairments and ways in which these impairments can be shown.

When an autistic spectrum disorder is present together with any other type of disability, the autism is a major factor in determining the programme of treatment that is needed. To take just a few examples, a child with Down's syndrome who has autism is different from other children with Down's syndrome and is unlikely to respond to the social group activities the others enjoy. A child with autism who is very overactive may not respond to medication that helps children with ADHD, and can be helped only if the autism is recognised. People with visual or hearing impairments need specialised help if they also have an autistic disorder. An adult with an autistic spectrum disorder who has visual hallucinations may be diagnosed as having a psychosis or schizophrenia, but may respond badly to the medication given for these conditions. Recognising the autism and providing the appropriate structured environment and programme of activities is much more likely to alleviate the hallucinations and 'psychotic' behaviour.

Because it is so important to detect any underlying autistic disorder, professionals whose work brings them into contact with children or adults with these conditions need to be alert to the possibility of multiple diagnosis or misdiagnosis. It is also important to recognise when aspects of a child's problems are not due to autism but to an associated disorder, such as seizures, which may respond to medical treatment. Professionals involved should have training in methods of history-taking and observation that can reveal an underlying autistic disorder, or know where to refer to a clinician who is experienced in the field.

Understanding the nature of autistic spectrum disorders

- Children and adults with autistic spectrum disorders have little or no spontaneous social feeling for other people, not even for their own parents.
- They gradually develop a need for their familiar carers but this takes time.
- Parents, teachers, carers and other professionals involved have to learn how to interact with children and adults with this special developmental pattern.
- This is strange and different from the usual experience of social interaction with non-autistic people, whether or not they have disabilities.
- However, many people involved personally or professionally find working with people with these conditions deeply rewarding.

Parents, carers, teachers and other professionals need to understand and sympathise with the nature of autistic spectrum disorders and the way in which people with these conditions experience the world. If people living and working with individuals with autistic spectrum disorders do not have the requisite knowledge, they tend to interpret the odd behaviour in terms with which they are familiar, such as deliberate naughtiness, laziness or, in adults in a psychiatric setting, schizophrenia or other psychosis. This leads to inappropriate management and treatment, especially the misuse of medication. Treatment-resistant schizophrenia is one of the diagnoses that can be wrongly given to an adult with an autistic spectrum disorder. Improved autism awareness among professionals may help prevent misdiagnoses of this kind.

Meeting the special needs

Making the world understandable

- Use clear, simple methods of communicating, adapted to the level of ability of the person concerned.
- Make abstract ideas concrete through visual demonstration.
- Provide an organised, predictable structure for each day and a programme of activities adapted to the individual concerned.
- Use special interests to encourage development of a wider range of activities.
- Have a calm, confident, patient, detached, unemotional, low-key approach combined with genuine positive feelings for the person concerned.

Children and adults with autism need people to communicate with them in clear and easily understandable ways. Speaking clearly and concisely and using visual prompts to illustrate what you are saying can help. Complex, shifting ideas like the unwritten rules of social life need to be explained in concrete terms, with the use of visual illustrations.

People with autistic spectrum disorders tend to need more time than usual to process incoming information and cope better if the people interacting with them are patient, unemotional and objective. They function best if they have a structured, organised, predictable programme of daily activities and a calm, ordered environment. The rules of daily life need to be listed explicitly in visual form and should be followed by everyone involved, not just the person with an autistic disorder.

Life is puzzling, confusing and often frightening for people with autistic spectrum disorders. Allowing and encouraging each person to develop their special skills and interests, as long as these are not in any way dangerous or distressing to others, improves their quality of life. Experience, tact and empathy are needed by carers to ensure that the special interests can be followed but do not take over the whole life of the person concerned. In the past, some professionals in the field have advocated refusing to allow any repetitive activity, including special interests. Experience has shown that this causes distress and, if anything, exacerbates the autistic disorder. With the right approach, special interests can sometimes be used as a starting point for wider interests. For example, a childhood fascination with water pipes may lead to working as a plumber in adult life.

Organising the environment

- A calm, quiet, well-organised environment 'with a place for everything and everything in its place' is the ideal.
- Noise and other sensory stimuli need to be kept at as low a level as possible, especially for those children and adults who are oversensitive to different kinds of sensory input.
- Small groups which allow for individual attention are needed.
- The choice of appropriate companions in a residential group of people with autistic spectrum disorders can be a crucial factor for success.

For all people with autism, whether at home, school, in an adult centre or at work, it helps if the environment is organised, predictable and as calm as possible. Those living or working with people with autistic spectrum disorders need to be aware of any oversensitivity to sound, smell, touch or other sensory input and to take the necessary action to reduce exposure to the sensations that cause distress. If there are catatonic and parkinsonian features, carers need to have experience with the non-medical aspects of helping, including techniques of gentle prompting and avoidance of pressurising the person concerned to carry out tasks that they find difficult. These methods are important even if medication is prescribed.

The best way to reduce or even prevent aggressive, destructive, or self-injurious behaviour is to provide the right kind of help and education and to organise the environment using the principles briefly outlined above. The development of skills in ways that can be generalised, which will help the young person to manage anxiety and cope in a wide range of settings in later life, should also be part of the school curriculum and will require highly skilled teaching.

For many individuals with challenging behaviour and/or severe learning disabilities, the appropriate help can be obtained only in a setting that is specially organised for people with autistic spectrum disorders. They will need this type of setting for all of their lives.

Education

- Children with autistic spectrum disorders behave and learn in ways that differ profoundly from those with typical development.
- They should be taught social skills and skills that will help them to cope with and manage anxiety.
- Teaching should also focus on developing skills in ways that can be generalised to a wide range of settings or uses.
- Many find mainstream school intensely distressing.
- Specialist schools are essential for those who cannot cope with mainstream. These should include some offering boarding facilities.
- Appropriate training in autistic spectrum disorders for teachers and other professionals in specialist or mainstream schools is essential.

Children with autistic spectrum disorders benefit from education tailored to their needs and level of ability. Specialist schools as well as inclusion, with support, in mainstream schools are required. The fundamental problem is that the way children with autistic disorders behave and the way they learn are so different from their typically developing peers. Due to the nature of their difficulties, particularly with social interaction or sensory sensitivities, so-called 'integration' in mainstream school can cause many problems for some children, even if they have a high level of ability and are given support. Those who find mainstream school stressful may be disruptive in class. Another pattern often seen is the child who is quiet and undemanding at school but displays challenging behaviour at home, as the stress of the day is released there.

Careful assessment of each child's educational needs followed by appropriate provision is essential if children with autism are to improve in behaviour and make progress. When making assessments, the purpose of attending school should be borne in mind. Every child is entitled to an education, the aim of which is to help the child to achieve his or her highest potential. Some children with autism 'cope' in mainstream school because they cause no problems, but learn little or nothing from the experience.

Some, but by no means all, the people with autistic spectrum disorders who do not have associated learning difficulties or challenging behaviour do make progress in mainstream schools if given appropriate support and, as adults, achieve some degree of independence in living or working. Even this group find life hard and have to strive continually to behave in socially acceptable ways – an effort most tend to find very tiring. Unless they find a friend with similar interests or a social group they can join, they may lead lonely lives. Those who do best have the type of temperament that allows them to accept themselves and find contentment in following their special interests.

The attitudes of teachers, classmates and learning support assistants can make a great difference. Education of the educators is a key factor. It would be of great value if, in their training, teachers could learn about autistic spectrum disorders and ways of helping children with ASDs to cope in school. A teacher's understanding approach to children with autistic spectrum disorders in mainstream school could have a positive effect on the attitudes of other children, which, it is to be hoped, would last into adult life. Clare Sainsbury, in her talk to the NAS annual general meeting in 2002, said, "People at the high-functioning end of the spectrum may need different types of support – and we may need much lower levels of support to enable us to succeed – but we are often no less dependent on that support than anyone else [on the spectrum]."

Occupation and leisure

- After leaving school, those who are unable to become independent need daily access to structured, organised activities that fit with their level of ability and special interests.
- Many adults who are able to work need help in finding an appropriate occupation and support when learning the job.
- Many young adults need help to develop realistic expectations for their future.

After leaving school, people with autistic spectrum disorders need regular occupation and leisure pursuits. Without a daily timetable of appropriate activities there is a high chance of loss of utilisation of skills and deterioration in behaviour. Facilities available in the community, such as those provided by further education colleges, leisure centres, horse riding and other outdoor pursuits have proved beneficial and enjoyable for many people with autistic spectrum disorders. However, most also need access to day centres with special expertise in working with people with autism. One of the most important aspects of such centres is the training of staff. As well as working in the centres, staff can support people with autistic spectrum disorders when taking part in activities in the community.

Many of the more able adults with autistic spectrum disorders do find regular, paid employment. Some cope well but others experience difficulties from time to time. For example, they may do so well at their routine work that they are promoted to posts that require more flexibility and interaction with others, which their social impairment makes difficult or impossible. They need skilled support from professional workers who can explain to employers the type of work people with autistic spectrum disorders can and cannot do. The National Autistic Society runs a supported employment scheme, Prospects, which helps people with Asperger syndrome to find and keep suitable jobs. Prospects employment advisers help employers to understand people with Asperger syndrome as well as supporting the people themselves through initial interviews and settling in to work.

While some cope well with work and even marriage, many of the more able adolescents and young adults have unrealistic expectations about their futures and expect to develop successful careers and relationships, including marriage and children. Evaluation[5] has confirmed that access to employment did improve wealth and independence but did not improve social relationships. Staff who are likely to come into contact with young people with autism, for example at colleges, adult centres or in the workplace, should receive training on helping people to come to terms with these difficulties, as they are a source of great anger, frustration and depression.

Accommodation

- Most adults who need residential care require small, specialist residential homes.

While some more able adults with autism are able to organise their own living accommodation, many live at home with their parents. This can work well, especially if support from professional workers is available. All too often, especially if they have no organised daily activities, the person concerned stays at home all day doing little or nothing. As a consequence, some make heavy demands on their ageing parents and may become verbally or physically aggressive. This can sometimes result in severe problems for the individual and their family.

Finding alternative residential accommodation is often a major problem. Adults with autistic spectrum disorders can be found in all types of sheltered accommodation, much of which is unsuitable. The most successful provision is accommodation that specialises in helping people with autistic spectrum disorders. The National Autistic Society, many local autism organisations, some other voluntary or private organisations and some local authorities have developed a range of specialised accommodation, varying from fully staffed residential homes to single-person flats with support staff available when needed.

Special needs of those with autistic spectrum disorder and ADHD and/or PDA

- Special experience and skill is needed to work with children and adults with these additional features.
- The aim is to provide a basic, firm structure but allow enough flexibility within the framework to sustain the interest of the child or adult concerned.

[5]Mawhood, L. and Howlin, P. (1999). The outcome of a supported employment scheme for high-functioning adults with autism or Asperger syndrome. *Autism*, 1999, Sep, Vol. 3(3), pp229-254

As noted previously, when one or both of these behaviour patterns is present in a child or adult with an autistic spectrum disorder, special problems arise because such children do not take kindly to a rigid routine. But, paradoxically, they need a secure structure in their environment and daily programme just as much as other people with autistic spectrum disorders. Programmes have to be designed for each individual but there are certain general principles. These include providing a basic structure for each day which is fixed, but allows for a wide choice of activities to be fitted into the basic timetable, and allowing lots of opportunity for different kinds of physical exercise.

Regarding staff support, it helps if the number of staff interacting with the person concerned is kept to a minimum. Staff should be at a senior level, experienced, mature, flexible and creative and remain calm, quiet and confident regardless of any provocation. In order to review progress and discuss any issues and ideas, a daily debrief at the end of every working day for each of the staff concerned is useful.

Involvement with the criminal justice system

- People with autistic spectrum disorders or their parents may become involved with the law.
- Police and other professionals involved need appropriate training.
- The laws concerned with disability should recognise the existence of autistic spectrum disorders and their effect on behaviour.

As mentioned previously, a small minority of people with autistic spectrum disorders, particularly those with the additional problems of PDA or ADHD, break the law – mainly because of their difficulty in coping with social situations and social relationships. The criminal justice system can also become involved with the families of children with autistic conditions. The usual reason for this is that the autism has not been recognised and the parents have been blamed for the child's unusual behaviour. The police and other professionals involved need to have at least enough training to recognise that an autistic spectrum disorder may be present, and to know where to turn for expert advice. Research carried out by nfpSynergy for The National Autistic Society in 2005 found that 92 per cent of police officers and 94 per cent of solicitors questioned had not received autism training. In response to this, the NAS launched a criminal justice awareness campaign and published *Autism: a guide for criminal justice professionals*[6], an information pack tailored to the needs of criminal justice professionals.

The law as it stands is not equipped to understand the nature of autistic spectrum disorders. If the courts become involved for either of the above reasons ill-informed judgements can be made, sometimes with disastrous consequences. It would be helpful if the law relating to disability was able to take into account the effect of developmental disorders, such as autistic spectrum conditions, on behaviour.

---

[6]The National Autistic Society (2005). *Autism: a guide for criminal justice professionals*. London: The National Autistic Society. Available to download from The National Autistic Society's website: www.autism.org.uk/cjp

Medication

- There is no medication that can alleviate or 'cure' the developmental impairments that underlie autistic disorders.
- Medication is used to treat associated conditions such as epilepsy and ADHD.
- The effects of medication are hard to predict and are sometimes paradoxical.
- Careful monitoring and discontinuation of medication which has no effect, or a detrimental effect, are essential.

Medical intervention is placed last in this section because understanding the nature of autistic spectrum disorders and the provision of a structured, organised environment and daily timetable are the most important ways of helping. Medication does have a place, but its role is limited and its use presents a number of special problems.

There is as yet no medication that can cure or even alleviate the impairments that underlie autistic spectrum disorders. Appropriate drugs can be used to treat associated conditions such as epilepsy. Medication is often tried in order to treat associated conditions that are suspected to be present, such as ADHD, Tourette syndrome, obsessive compulsive disorder, or some psychiatric illnesses. The problem is that symptoms similar to those seen in these conditions can occur as part of the autistic picture, making differential diagnosis difficult.

When medication is tried because an associated condition is suspected, the effects should be monitored with care and the medication stopped or another one tried if there is no change or if undesirable side-effects occur.

Problems are most likely to occur when medication is used with the aim of reducing behaviour such as aggression, agitation or self-injury. Sometimes the drugs used prove helpful, but often they are ineffective or produce undesirable side-effects. In some cases such large doses are given that people become sedated. This may stop the undesirable behaviour but severely reduces the quality of life of the person concerned. Again, careful attention to factors in the environment and a structured daily programme is required to improve both behaviour and quality of life.

There are some adults with autistic spectrum disorders who, in the past, were misdiagnosed as having a psychiatric illness and were given neuroleptic medication. Others were prescribed such drugs because of their challenging behaviour. They have been given this medication over many years, perhaps with increases in dosage. If and when the correct diagnosis is made and it is quite clear that the medication is ineffective or actually harmful, it is difficult to decide the best course of action. Stopping or even gradually reducing the neuroleptic can lead to both behavioural and physical side-effects, which may last for some time or even continue permanently. Changing to one of the newer neuroleptics may help but there is no guarantee. A plan of action for each individual has to be worked out by professionals with wide experience in this field and agreed with care staff, the family, if involved, and – if possible – with the person themselves.

Helping and supporting parents

- Most distressing for parents is the young child's inability to engage in reciprocal social interaction and communication.
- Diagnosis may be delayed for many years or never made at all.
- Parents often have to discover by trial and error how to understand and help their child.
- The demands of a child with an autistic spectrum disorder often conflict with the needs of typically developing siblings.
- Finding the right help and support and appropriate services may be a struggle.
- Early diagnosis, training of professionals, support and advice for parents and provision of appropriate services are key to helping children and adults with autistic spectrum disorders.

Most parents are totally unprepared for the shock of finding that they have a child with an autistic spectrum disorder. The diagnosis is rarely made before the second year of life and is often delayed for many years, up to adolescence or beyond; in some cases it is never made at all. Many, though not all, parents suspect from early in the first year that development is not proceeding along typical lines, but it is still deeply distressing when the diagnosis is finally made.

Mothers, fathers and the rest of the family have to come to terms with the lack of reciprocal social interaction and communication that gives such pleasure when engaged in by a typically developing young child and is the basis for a secure, happy parent-child relationship. They have to completely re-adjust their way of relating to their child. The natural behaviour of parents has to be modified to cope with a child who lacks any innate social instinct. Most parents have to find ways of coping the hard way through daily experience of living with their child. They have to learn the right way to respond to the child's strange and difficult behaviour, to discover the triggers for this behaviour and how they can be avoided. They have to learn how to help their child make sense of a frightening world, while living with their own fears for their child's future. Despite all these problems, most parents become very closely attached to the child with an autistic disorder, perhaps sensing early in the child's life his inability to cope with the world.

Even if the correct diagnosis is eventually made, parents will need energy and patience to obtain the appropriate education, medical and other services that are needed. They will experience different kinds of difficulties in living with their child and in finding appropriate services at each stage of their child's life. The problems vary in nature depending on the severity of the child's disability but life with a high-functioning child can be even harder than one with a child who is severely disabled. To add to all this, a family with one child with autism has a higher than average chance of having a second who is also on the spectrum. At the same time, the needs of any typically developing siblings still have to be met.

Parents need to have a diagnosis as early as possible. They require expert help and support in order to understand their child and to help their child develop to his fullest potential. Up to the present, most parents have found that few professionals they have encountered have had any useful knowledge of autistic spectrum disorders. This situation is now changing with the increasing awareness of autism and the provision of professional training courses, but there is still a long way to go.

Ideally, all those in relevant professions, such as health and education professionals, should learn about developmental disorders, including autistic spectrum conditions, in their professional training. Books, magazines and other materials intended for new parents should contain useful, practical information on these conditions as well as typical development. Appropriate information and support for the parents is one of the most important ways of helping both the children concerned and the whole family. National and local autism societies and related voluntary bodies are a valuable resource for families.

Prevalence

- About six to seven and possibly as many as nine in every 1,000 have some kind of autistic spectrum disorder.
- About two or three in every 1,000 have mild or severe learning disabilities and almost all of these will need care all their lives.
- It is not known how many people with an IQ over 70 will need help and support, nor for how long, nor at what times in their lives. Some achieve independence as adults, others do not.
- The apparent increase in the number of people with autism is due to changes in diagnostic criteria and increased awareness.
- There are no reliable prevalence figures for adults but it should be remembered that children with autism become adults with autism; a number are diagnosed for the first time in adulthood, their difficulties having been missed or misdiagnosed as children or adolescents.

The first epidemiological studies used Kanner and Eisenberg's[7] very strict criteria for classic autism and found age-specific rates of around four to five in every 10,000 children. Autism was therefore considered to be a rare condition. Since then, with the development of the concept of the autistic spectrum, the criteria have become much wider. Current estimates suggest approximately six to seven and possibly as many as nine in every 1,000 have some kind of autistic spectrum disorder. Of these, about two or three in every 1,000 have mild or severe learning disabilities, that is, IQ under 70. Most if not all those who have learning disabilities will need care throughout their lives.

Among people who are in the borderline, average or high range of ability, it is more difficult to calculate prevalence, how many will still need care and how many will become independent in adult life. Autistic spectrum disorders shade into typical development without a neat boundary. Rough estimates suggest that around four to five and possibly up to seven people in every 1,000 have a high-functioning autistic spectrum disorder. Perhaps half or more of these will achieve independence in living and/or working. Even these, however, need special understanding and support during childhood, particularly in secondary school when they are preparing to make the important transition from school to adult life.

Those who do not achieve independence as adults will need some degree of support throughout their lives. Parents often provide this, frequently sacrificing their own quality of life. Eventually, when parents are no longer able to cope, the health or social services will have to take over the responsibility. When they do this, it is crucial that they have a good understanding of appropriate service provision for people with autistic spectrum disorders.

The lesson from the current studies of the epidemiology of autistic disorders is that they are not rare conditions. Some people believe that there has been a recent dramatic rise in the numbers of children with autism – an 'autism epidemic'. However, there is good evidence that there has been no real change in numbers.

---

[7]Kanner, L. and Eisenberg, L. (1956). Early infantile autism 1943-1955. *American Journal of Orthopsychiatry*, 26, pp55-65

The apparent rise is due, mostly if not entirely, to wider diagnostic criteria, more awareness among parents and professionals, and the realisation that autism can occur together with other disabilities and with any level of ability.

One factor that may possibly have led to some real rise in prevalence is the very considerable decrease in infant mortality and the recent, marked increase in the survival rate of very premature babies. There is as yet no evidence of an association between infant mortality rate and identification of autistic disorders but the possibility needs to be investigated.

Implications for services

- There are many adults with autistic spectrum disorders in day or residential services of all kinds who have never been properly diagnosed.
- There are many adults with autistic spectrum disorders who are unknown to services but who need help.
- The current ICD-10/DSM-IV criteria may mean that people are excluded from the services they need.
- IQ levels are also used to exclude people from services they need.
- As more people receive a diagnosis, more will need access to appropriate support; therefore continued funding and development of autism-specific services for both adults and children is important.

The increase in the numbers of children and adults being diagnosed with an autistic spectrum disorder does not mean that large numbers of people with severe disabilities are appearing who have never contacted services before. The epidemiological studies have shown that most of these have been in touch with various different kinds of services but, in many cases, the nature of their underlying problems has not, in the past, been recognised.

In the first half of the 20th century many of those with learning disabilities and/or challenging behaviour would have been living in large institutions but not diagnosed as having autism. The implication of the correct epidemiological findings is that there are large numbers of adults of all ages with autistic spectrum disorders who have never been diagnosed and whose special needs are not recognised.

The situation for high-functioning adults is somewhat different. Many will have achieved some degree of independence and may not have been in contact with services. However, an unknown number struggle with psychological or psychiatric problems and a poor quality of life because their special needs are not recognised. Some adults have contacted The National Autistic Society's Centre for Social and Communication Disorders in middle or even old age because they have, by chance, read an article that describes their problems clearly and has given them a name for their condition.

As already discussed, whatever way the triad is manifested, whatever their level of ability and whatever other features or associated conditions are present, people with autistic spectrum disorders have certain special needs that differ from those of other groups. The wide range of manifestations can make it difficult for a child or, more especially, for an adult to obtain help from the education, health, learning disability or social services. All of these services are involved in providing for people with autistic spectrum disorders. All too often the boundaries set by each make it difficult for those on the borderlines to obtain the appropriate help.

Likewise, the current ICD-10/DSM-IV criteria, which can be used to decide which services are appropriate for people, do not cover everyone on the autistic spectrum. For example, using these criteria, children and adults with ability in the average or high range may not be recognised as having a developmental disorder. This may be the case even though they may have marked social impairment and be in need of help.

At the other end of the spectrum, children and adults with severe learning disabilities may not be recognised as having an autistic spectrum disorder, despite their lack of interest or pleasure in even the most simple social interaction. This lack of interest may be explained away as being due to their very low level of development. They may then be denied the specially organised environment and understanding carers they require.

Another problem is that an adult with an autistic spectrum disorder whose overall IQ is in the average range, but who has low levels of social skills, may be excluded from services for people with learning disabilities that would be helpful. They may instead be referred to the mental health services, even though such services often have nothing useful to offer people with autistic spectrum disorders.

Someone else with an autistic spectrum disorder may also have a mental illness, such as depression. If they are referred to mental health services, the underlying autistic spectrum disorder may not be recognised or it may be discounted, even though it should be taken into consideration when planning treatment and ongoing support. A person who has an autistic spectrum disorder, a learning disability and a mental illness presents yet another dilemma for the statutory services. Furthermore, as parents know all too well, the division between children's and adults' services creates problems when people with an ASD try to make the transition from one type of service to another.

Integrated or specialised services?

- Integrated education and other services are appropriate for some but many have bad experiences in such settings.
- The preferences of the child or adult for an integrated or specialist service should be carefully considered and acted upon.
- Specialist services should be seen as a positive first choice providing optimum conditions for development of potential – not a last resort.
- Many admissions to high-cost, secure services could have been prevented had access to appropriate specialist services been made available.
- Specialist schools and adult services with well-trained staff are needed in all parts of the country.

Children and adults with autistic spectrum disorders can be found in every kind of education, health and social service. In the past, before autism was recognised, there was no guarantee of appropriate care and support. The type of care many people received exacerbated rather than reduced their difficulties. In 1962, The National Autistic Society was set up with the specific aim of opening special schools designed for children with autistic spectrum disorders. Despite the ideologically driven belief that all disabled people should be integrated into mainstream services, the NAS and other bodies concerned with autistic disorders have continued to develop specialised services because they are acutely aware of the need for them. A study by the NAS, *Inclusion and autism: is it working?*[8], showed that people with autistic disorders are much more likely than other groups to be excluded from mainstream schools and other services.

[8]Barnard, J., Prior, A., and Potter, D. (2000). *Inclusion and autism: is it working?* London: The National Autistic Society. Available to download from The National Autistic Society's website: www.autism.org.uk/inclusionreport

In addition to schools, the NAS has developed specialised diagnostic services, information and support for parents, sheltered employment, a scheme to support and help adults to settle in open employment, various kinds of living accommodation, specialised group and individual counselling, and a residential forensic unit for those whose social impairment has led them into trouble with the law. The success of these schemes in helping those whom integration into mainstream services has failed demonstrates that both specialised and integrated services are required so that the needs of each individual can be met. There is a particular need for increasing the numbers of specialist residential schools, including some that provide accommodation for 52 weeks of the year.

Ideally, the education, social and health services and the police and criminal justice systems should formally recognise the existence of autistic spectrum disorders. People who, during their professional lives, are likely to come in to contact with those with autistic spectrum disorders should have appropriate training. It should be recognised that a flexible approach is important. For example, if a person with autism with a high IQ would best be helped by the learning disability services, the IQ level should not necessarily be a barrier to providing for the person's needs. It should also be accepted that, while integration is appropriate for some, others need specialist services at some, if not all, stages of their lives.

The need to maintain appropriate service provision

- When a person with an autistic spectrum disorder, who is dependent on the help of services, is placed in a structured, organised environment that suits them well, improvement in skills and behaviour often occurs over time.

If a person with autism does well in a supported environment, the authorities may make the assumption that their problems are 'cured' and move the person concerned to a less organised, more mixed environment. In many, if not most such cases, the consequence is relapse back to the original problems or worse. The lesson is that autistic spectrum disorders cannot be cured and are very markedly affected by the environment. Any attempt to 'move on' someone who has coped well in one setting has to be thought through with great care, monitored closely and reversed if a relapse occurs.

Evaluating interventions

- Independent evaluation of unproven claims for interventions for autistic spectrum disorders is urgently required.

There is no known curative treatment for autistic disorders but many claims have been made for the efficacy of a variety of approaches. Authorities providing services can be faced with demands to provide expensive 'therapies' of unproven value. There is a need for independent evaluation to ensure the development of good practice and better use of available resources. Research Autism, an independent charity associated with The National Autistic Society, has been set up to facilitate independent evaluation and to give parents and professionals easy access to all the available objective information.

Staff training

- Specialist training for all professionals who are involved with children or adults with autistic spectrum disorders is essential.
- Co-operation between professionals and parents or other carers is important.

Staff working with people with autistic spectrum disorders need training, especially in the specific areas related to understanding and responding to autism. Good, up-to-date theoretical understanding leading to informed practice is essential to underpin the approaches and organisation of services. It is important for staff to know *why* they need to behave in certain ways.

Professionals have to know how to work in partnership with parents to ensure good communication and consistency of approach. This is as important for those working with adults as it is for children, as long as the parents remain involved with their son or daughter. Professionals and parents both need to understand and empathise with the problems experienced by each group. Each must resist the temptation to blame the other when things go wrong. Co-operation in looking for the cause of any challenging behaviour is much more likely to lead to a solution of the problems.

Conclusions

The problem of resources will always be with us. However, the resources that are available could be used more efficiently if it were recognised that autistic spectrum disorders occur in a very wide range of manifestations, but that they all have in common special features that make them different from other types of disabilities, whatever other condition may be present.

Specialised training of carers and other professionals is essential. One of the most important results emerging from an NAS survey of its members, sent out in spring 2004, is that most improvement in the behaviour and skills of people with autistic disorders was not produced by any specific medications or approaches. Most improvement occurred when the professionals concerned developed, through training and experience, an understanding of autism, a realisation of the need to focus on strengths rather than deficits, and genuine empathy with the child or adult concerned.

People with autistic spectrum disorders have many positive qualities. Many of those who are high-functioning, despite their difficulties, have made remarkable contributions to society by using their special gifts in the arts or sciences. Without them, the world would be a poorer place. Appropriate provision of services which offer the specialised help and support people with autistic spectrum disorders need can enable them to overcome their problems and use their gifts.

For those who are more severely disabled, their quality of guileless innocence can touch the heart of the most cynical 'neurotypical' (the name invented by people with Asperger syndrome for those outside the autistic spectrum!). The aim must be to make their lives as happy and contented as possible.

Further reading

* Brown, M. and Miller, A. (2004). *Aspects of Asperger's: success in the teens and twenties.* Bristol: Lucky Duck Publishing

* Deudney, C. (2004). *Mental health in people with autism and Asperger syndrome.* London: The National Autistic Society

Frith, U. (ed.) (1991). *Autism and Asperger syndrome.* Cambridge: Cambridge University Press

Jordan, R. and Jones, G. (1999). *Meeting the needs of children with autistic spectrum disorders.* London: David Fulton Publishers

* May, F. (2005). *Understanding behaviour.* London: The National Autistic Society

Medical Research Council (2002). *MRC review of autism research.* London: MRC

* Prospects Supported Employment Team (2005). *The undiscovered workforce – employing people with Asperger syndrome: a practical guide.* London: The National Autistic Society

* Vermeulen, P. (2001). *Autistic thinking: this is the title.* London: Jessica Kingsley Publishers

* Whitaker, P. (2001). *Challenging behaviour and autism.* London: The National Autistic Society

* Wilkes, K. (2005). *The sensory world of the autistic spectrum.* London: The National Autistic Society

* Wing, L. (1996). *The autistic spectrum: a guide for parents and professionals.* London: Constable and Robinson

Real-life accounts

* Fleisher, M. (2003). *Making sense of the unfeasible: my life journey with Asperger syndrome.* London: Jessica Kingsley Publishers

* Gerland, G. (1997). *A real person: life on the outside.* London: Souvenir Press

* Jackson, L. (2002). *Freaks, geeks and Asperger syndrome.* London: Jessica Kingsley Publishers

* Sainsbury, C. (2000). *Martian in the playground: understanding the schoolchild with Asperger's syndrome.* Bristol: Lucky Duck Publishing

* These titles are available to order from The National Autistic Society. To order, telephone our suppliers on 0845 458 9911 or visit our website: www.autism.org.uk/pubs